OUTER SPACE ADVENTURES

Written by: Alba Arboleda
Laura Cohen
Tina Harris
Project Manager: Ann de la Sota
Consulting Editors: Emilie Ferry
Lucy Vezzuto, Ph.D.

Table of Contents

Skywatch

Come to a stargazing party and see what's visible in the night sky.

On a very clear night the sky seems crowded with countless glittering dots of light. If you know where to look and what to look for, you can see many stars and planets with just your eyes. Many other space objects, because of their distance from the Earth, can only be seen with an Earth-based telescope. Still other objects are totally invisible to our eyes.

Below is a list of some objects in the night sky. Imagine that you are standing at the best possible place on Earth, on just the right night, at the perfect time to see these objects. You have to decide whether each item would be:

○ Visible to the naked eye
△ Invisible
□ Visible with an Earth-based telescope

1. North Star
2. Venus
3. Black Hole
4. Neptune
5. Stars of the Big Dipper
6. Earth's Moon
7. X rays
8. Constellation Orion
9. Radio Waves
10. Pluto

Stargazer's Guide

VISIBLE TO THE NAKED EYE

North Star
The North Star marks the tail-end of the Little Dipper. Also called Polaris, it is the most important star in the heavens because it is used by navigators.

Venus
The second planet closest to the Sun, Venus is brighter than any other nighttime object except the Moon. In the Northern Hemisphere, during September, it is in the east sky. In December Venus can easily be seen in the southwest sky.

Big Dipper
The Big Dipper is one of the easiest star groups to find. It looks like a water dipper with a long handle and points the way to Polaris. Just follow the two stars in the front of the dipper's cup . . . they point right to Polaris!

Earth's Moon
The Moon is the closest and brightest object in our night sky. Because it revolves around the Earth, there are times when we can't see it.

Constellation Orion
From the Northern Hemisphere, Orion is seen best when you face the south sky. You can see four stars in a box shape with three stars clustered in a row in the middle. These clustered stars have been called Orion's "belt buckle."

VISIBLE WITH AN EARTH-BASED TELESCOPE

Neptune
From now until 1999, Neptune will be the planet that is farthest away from the sun. It is a very cold planet.

Pluto
Pluto has an oval orbit, and right now it is closer to the sun than Neptune is. By 1999 it will again be the farthest planet from the sun. Scientists can only see this relatively small planet with a powerful telescope.

INVISIBLE

Black Hole
A black hole emits powerful beams of x rays. Any matter that gets near its center is pulled into the hole. Not even light can escape its strong pull!

X rays
X rays are a form of invisible light. Many objects in the universe give off x rays. These rays can only be detected with special space-based satellites.

Radio waves
These signals come from some of the stars in our galaxy. Detected only by a radio telescope, radio waves pulsate from certain stars called pulsars.

On Your Own

Call or write your nearest observatory. Ask which planets can be seen in your sky right now and how to find them! (Some observatories have tape-recorded stargazer messages.)

Answers

Danger Ahead!

Watch out for meteoroids! Duck the space debris! Help rescue a crippled spacecraft without endangering your own craft and crew.

Exploring the frontiers of space can be risky. Astronauts face many potential dangers—equipment breakdowns, exposure to dangerous radiation, or collisions with space debris. Just entering and leaving Earth's atmosphere can pose a serious threat to life. A spacecraft must provide backup systems and protective equipment in case of any emergency.

Below is a list of safety and space-rescue equipment. Can you tell which piece of equipment is described by each of the ten sentences at the right?

A. Meteoroid shield
B. Nosecap and thermal protection shield
C. Restraint harness system
D. Personal rescue enclosure
E. Automatic navigator
F. Storm cellar
G. Sunshade
H. Orbital maneuvering system
I. Secondary oxygen pack
J. Manipulator arm

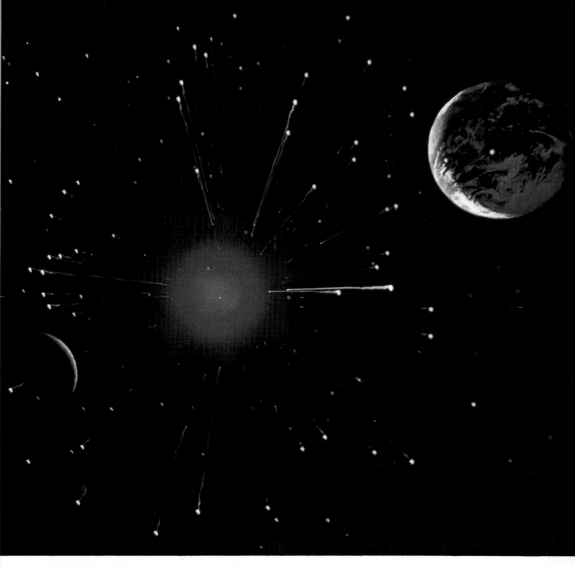

1. What simple device keeps an astronaut from being thrown about a shuttle cabin?
   ○ B   □ C

2. A spacecraft's strong outer skin protects it from heat and the impact of small space rocks. What is this protective "skin" called?
   ○ A   □ H

3. If a spaceship's meteoroid shield is destroyed, what can be used to block solar rays from overheating a spacecraft?
   ○ F   □ G

4. What would an astronaut use if his or her primary oxygen tank failed during a spacewalk?
   ○ A   □ I

5. In an emergency, a crew member without a spacesuit would be towed to safety in a special capsule. What is it called?
   ○ D   □ C

6. What mechanical device is used by astronauts to make repairs to the outside of the shuttle without leaving the craft?
   ○ D   □ J

7. What does a shuttle pilot use to make emergency changes of speed or direction to avoid dangerous space debris?
   ○ A   □ H

8. What can astronauts climb into for protection from solar storm radiation?
   ○ I   □ F

9. What protects a spacecraft from burning up as it re-enters Earth's atmosphere?
   ○ B   □ G

10. What on-board computer can be set to guide the shuttle's re-entry and landing on Earth?
    ○ E   □ J

Shuttlenauts Sam and Orba set off for an important rescue mission. They must bring the crew of a crippled spacecraft safely to Earth.

We'd better fasten our *restraint harnesses.*

Roger.

Breaking free of Earth's atmosphere, the duo heads into deep space.

Meteor shower dead ahead!

Let's engage the *orbital maneuvering system.* If we shift direction, we'll miss most of those flying rocks!

On Your Own

Create a space adventure comic strip of your own. Collect space travel facts at your local library. Use your imagination to create interesting characters and an action-packed story line.

We've been hit!

Relax. Our *meteoroid shield* can take it.

Whew! There's not much damage. I'll use the *manipulator arm* to repair one of our cameras.

Meanwhile, the crew of the crippled Cosmos waits for rescue within the radiation-proof walls of the shuttle's *storm cellar.*

Not even a *sunshade* can keep us from overheating now.

I hope a rescue team arrives soon!

Answers

 Sam calling Cosmos. We're coming to get you! Hop into your *personal rescue enclosures!*

On our way! Wait, got a problem. Primary oxygen tank malfunctioning. Can't breathe. Switching to *secondary oxygen pack.*

You okay, Orba?

No problem. Let's welcome our guests.

Prepare for atmospheric interface; we're almost home.

The computer-directed *automatic navigator* will take us down.

How about a pizza when we get in?

I'm buying!

Sam and Orba head back to Earth with their new friends. The shuttle's *nosecap* and *thermal protection shield* safeguard them from burning up as they re-enter Earth's atmosphere.

Astronomical Numbers

Check these way-out numbers to find the mega-mistakes.

Did you know that in just 15 years, between 1917 and 1932, the size of the known Universe expanded one trillion times (1,000,000,000,000)? That's right—one trillion has twelve zeros. Today's scientists have no problem working with such astronomical numbers. However, for most of us, so many zeros can be quite confusing.

To the right are some fascinating facts about our Universe. Some of the numbers were written incorrectly and do not match the number words. Which numerals are written correctly and which are not? For each fact, decide if the number words and numerals in parentheses:

○ Match
☐ Do not match

1. The odds against being hit by a falling meteor are **ten trillion** (10,000,000,000,000) to one.

2. The Earth completes its **585-million** (585,000) mile orbit around the Sun in 365 days. That's about eight times faster than a speeding bullet.

3. A nine pound baby would weigh **ninety billion** (90,000,000) pounds on the surface of a neutron star.

4. Scientists estimate that the Sun has enough energy to keep shining for another **ten billion** (10,000,000,000) years.

5. We have proof there are at least **one sextillion** (1,000,000,000,000,000,000,000) stars in the Milky Way . . . and we're still counting!

6. Scientists have figured that the Sun is **four billion, six hundred million** (4,600,000) years old.

7. The Sun is **three million** (3,000,000) miles closer to the Earth during winter than summer.

8. Traveling at a speed of **one hundred eighty-six thousand** (186,000) miles per second, light takes six hours to travel from Pluto to Earth.

9. The size of the Universe is estimated at **two hundred ten sextillion** (210,000,000,000,000) miles.

10. The tail of a comet can extend **one hundred million** (100,000,000,000) miles across space.

100 MILLION MILES

Number Chart

Name	Number of Zeros	No. of Groups of Three 0's	Example
thousand	3	1	1,000
million	6	2	1,000,000
billion	9	3	1,000,000,000
trillion	12	4	1,000,000,000,000
quadrillion	15	5	1,000,000,000,000,000
quintillion	18	6	1,000,000,000,000,000,000
sextillion	21	7	1,000,000,000,000,000,000,000

The World's Largest Number

What is the world's largest number? It's an impossible question to answer because mathematicians say there is no limit to how high numbers can go. This is called infinity. Infinity means "without end."

The largest number named so far is the **googol** (GOO guhl). It's a 1 followed by one hundred zeros! Who named this number—a computer? No, the googol was named by the nine-year-old nephew of a mathematician.

A googol looks like this:
10,000,000,000,000,000,000,000,000,000,000,000, 000,000,000,000,000,000,000,000,000,000,000, 000,000,000,000,000,000,000,000,000. 000.

On Your Own

What would you name a number with 150 zeros? A number with 500 zeros? One thousand zeros? Make a list of the "number names" you create. Compare your names with names your friends create.

Answers

Space-age Work Clothes

Get dressed for work— in outer space!

A personal, soft spacecraft built for one—that's the shuttle space suit! Called an Extravehicular Mobility Unit (EMU), the suit has been carefully designed to meet every basic human need. It provides oxygen to breathe and regulates body temperature. It gives protection from the freezing cold of space and the fierce heat of the sun's direct rays. Without this special suit, an astronaut would quickly perish. Extravehicular Activities (EVA), such as making shuttle or satellite repairs, would not be possible.

You are assigned to make repairs outside your shuttle. Put on your EMU and check to see that all its special parts are functioning properly before you venture outside the shuttle.

Below are listed ten parts of an EMU. Each part has a specific function, listed on the right. For each function, choose the letter of the part that performs that function.

A. Liquid cooling and ventilation garment
B. Primary life support subsystem
C. Secondary oxygen pack
D. Insuit drink bag
E. EVA checklist
F. Communications carrier assembly
G. Television camera unit
H. Food bar
I. Helmet-mounted light array
J. Extravehicular visor assembly

1. Enables Mission Control on Earth to see live pictures from space
   ○ G   □ I
2. Purifies oxygen for breathing and adjusts water temperature
   ○ B   □ C
3. Circulates water through sewn-in tubes to regulate body heat
   ○ D   □ A
4. Carries back-up supply of oxygen
   ○ H   □ C
5. Details specific extravehicular missions to be performed on the flight
   ○ F   □ E
6. Supplies illumination for extravehicular activities in dark places
   ○ I   □ F
7. Shields astronaut's face from micrometeroids and radiation
   ○ E   □ J
8. Allows astronaut to talk with other crew members via microphones and earphones
   ○ F   □ G
9. Provides instant source of solid nourishment
   ○ H   □ D
10. Provides instant source of liquid nourishment
    ○ A   □ D

TV camera
The camera is mounted above the helmet to take pictures of what the astronaut sees.

Extravehicular visor assembly
This gold-coated shield snaps onto the outside of a helmet for protection from space debris.

Communications carrier assembly
Called the "Snoopy cap," it holds a miniature sound system under the helmet.

In-suit drink bag
This bag contains 22 ounces of juice or drinking water.

Secondary oxygen pack
This pack contains a 30-minute backup supply of oxygen.

Food bar
This foodstick of compressed fruit, grain, and nuts is wrapped in edible paper. It is placed near the astronaut's mouth.

Helmet-mounted light array
Small floodlights are built into the helmet attachment as an additional light source.

Primary life support subsystem
It contains a 7-hour oxygen supply and electrical power supply along with water tanks and a central cooling system.

EVA checklist
The checklist, mounted on the left forearm, lists information about how to perform extravehicular missions.

Liquid cooling and ventilation garment
This looks like long underwear. It has spaghetti-like tubes to circulate cooling water.

On Your Own

Someday many people will work in space. How will they tell each other apart in their similar spacesuits and helmets? Knights of old had different symbols on their shields. Design symbols these space workers could wear on their helmets for identification: coal miner, astronomer, medical researcher, and pilot.

Answers

The Astronomer's Attic

Use your observation powers! Detect what has been mysteriously moved in this astronomer's secret hideaway.

 rofessor Potter loves collecting instruments that astronomers used in the past. She keeps her prized possessions in the attic of her laboratory.

In the top picture, you can see the attic as it looked when Professor Potter went out this morning. While she was out, someone came in and moved several things around. Look carefully at the bottom picture. Compare each item with its placement in the picture. Then, decide if each item is either:

○ Changed in the bottom picture
□ Unchanged in the bottom picture

1. Telescope
2. Sky charts
3. Computer
4. Astrolabe
5. Sextant
6. Space station model
7. Space probe model
8. Model of solar system
9. Sky bowl
10. Videotape rack

Sky Bowl
A sky bowl shows the heavens as we see them from Earth. In a sky bowl we see where stars are in relation to each other, just as we see countries in relation to each other on a globe of Earth.

Astrolabe
(AZ truh layb)
The astrolabe was used by the ancient Greeks to measure the height and direction of objects in space. It was also used by sailors to guide their ships.

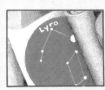

Sky Chart
A sky chart is like any other flat map; it shows where the stars are in the universe. By comparing the nighttime sky to an existing sky chart astronomers know when they have discovered a new star, or when a star has disappeared.

Computer
When scientists began work on space rockets in the 1950s, it was important that the math needed for the experiments be done quickly and correctly. The computer helped to calculate such things as the motion of the Earth and the correct speed of a rocket.

Model of Space Station
The first U.S. space station should be in orbit around the Earth by the year 2000. About 10 people will live and work on this space station.

Model of Solar System
Models of our solar system show each planet's position in relation to the Sun and the other planets.

Telescope
A telescope is made of a series of lenses that collect more light than your eyes can on their own. The lenses are curved to make the object you are observing appear larger.

Sextant
The sextant was invented in 1730. To use it, sailors pointed the sextant's telescope at the horizon. Then they moved an arm with a mirror attached along an arc marked with degrees. When the mirror reflected a known star along with the image of the horizon, the arc would show the sailors their degree of latitude and longitude.

On Your Own

If there was an auction of Professor Potter's instruments, which three would you most want to buy? Why?

Choose one of Professor Potter's instruments and read more about it in an encyclopedia or science book. Draw a diagram to show how it works.

Answers

Your Space Suitcase

Make plans for a fun-filled vacation in space! Pack your bags! What will you take?

oday, space travel is still quite new. Naturally, most space travelers so far have been astronauts, scientists and technicians. Soon, however, all kinds of different people will be able to go into space for work or vacations. Imagine conducting your own experiments aboard a shuttlecraft, or visiting the site of the first Moon landing!

What would you pack for a shuttle trip? Living in space is different from living on Earth. Some common household items are completely useless in space. Other things work as well in space as they do on Earth.

Decide whether or not each of these objects could be used inside a shuttlecraft in outer space.

○ Could be used
☐ Could not be used

1. Dart board and darts
2. Soft drink in a can
3. Record player
4. Jigsaw puzzle
5. Yo-yo
6. Jump rope
7. TV dinner
8. Magnetic chess set
9. Ball and jacks
10. Toothbrush and toothpaste

Can you think of a good experiment to conduct in space? The United States Space Agency wants students to suggest projects. Send your ideas to:
NASA Headquarters
Attn: Public Information
      Office
Washington, D.C. 20546.

Answers

Floating inside the zero gravity of a shuttlecraft can be fun, but weightlessness can pose some problems. For example, your soft drink would float around in a ball. Your TV dinner would fly about the cabin, creating a terrible mess! That's why specially designed food trays and liquid containers are used to make eating and drinking easier.

You would find your ball and jacks, jigsaw puzzles, record player, and jump rope useless. Without gravity, there is no up or down. Your ball would not drop and your jacks would disappear in every nook and cranny. Your jigsaw puzzle pieces wouldn't stay in place and your record would float off the turntable. Jumping rope wouldn't be much fun if your feet never touched the ground! A magnetic chess board will work, as will your yo-yo and dart set. In fact, it will be easier to play darts because, without gravity, they travel to the board in a straight line!

There's no getting around it—you'll still have to brush your teeth. Your toothpaste will stick to your brush because of its wetness. (But you'd better like its taste because you'll have to swallow it after brushing—or it'll float around after you spit it out.)

Way-out Wonders

Explore the weird and wonderful objects deep in outer space.

The Amateur Astronomy Club wants to decorate its clubhouse walls with some pictures of space wonders. One of the club members will do the painting while another will do the labeling.

Below is a list of ten space bodies that were painted for the walls of the clubhouse. Help the club members match the lettered objects on the right with their correct names. Hint: Some of these way-out wonders have very descriptive names.

1. White dwarf
   ○ J   ☐ F
2. Jupiter
   ○ I   ☐ G
3. Red supergiant star
   ○ E   ☐ H
4. Saturn
   ○ C   ☐ G
5. Comet
   ○ F   ☐ E
6. Spiral galaxy
   ○ G   ☐ E
7. Man-made satellite
   ○ I   ☐ D
8. Elliptical galaxy
   ○ C   ☐ B
9. Binary stars
   ○ J   ☐ B
10. Nebula
   ○ A   ☐ D

WHITE DWARF: After a star burns out it can become a white dwarf. It is called a dwarf because the star shrinks to a very small size.

JUPITER: This is the largest planet, 11 times larger than Earth. Colorful Jupiter has 16 moons and a Great Red Spot.

RED SUPERGIANT STAR: This largest kind of star can be a thousand times bigger than our Sun. It makes our sun look like a peanut!

SATURN: Gold-colored Saturn has 17 moons and many rings made of ice. It's no place for summer vacation. The temperature drops to -306 degrees F.

COMET: This "dirty snowball" contains small chunks of ice and dust. When a comet travels near the sun, the ice and dust layers shoot out to form a long glowing tail.

SPIRAL GALAXY: It's a huge collection of stars shaped like a pinwheel with arms coiling out from the center. Our galaxy, the Milky Way, is a spiral with some 400 billion stars.

MAN-MADE SATELLITE: This is a vehicle made by man to orbit the Earth, Moon, or other space bodies.

ELLIPTICAL GALAXY: Another type of galaxy, this collection of stars is shaped like an oval.

BINARY STARS: These double stars are inseparable! They revolve around each other.

NEBULA: A nebula (NEB yoo luh) is a large cloud of dust and gases found in a galaxy believed to be the result of a star explosion.

On Your Own

Imagine that you were the first scientist to see the space bodies described on this page. What descriptive name would you give each of them? Make a list of your names.

Answers

Planet Puzzlers

Take a fact-finding tour through our solar system, the home of the planets.

S pace exploration has led to many remarkable discoveries about the planets that revolve around our sun. Each new space mission brings us more amazing facts. Some of these facts prove what we've believed for centuries. Other facts provide us with new information that changes our thinking about the planets.

For each of the ten facts below, choose the letter of the planet or star that the fact describes. Use the picture of the solar system on the right for hints.

1. This planet has a pink daytime sky and a crystal-clear night sky.
   - ○ I
   - □ E
2. This is the only star in the solar system.
   - ○ A
   - □ C
3. This planet is farthest from the Sun.
   - ○ J
   - □ H
4. This planet was named after the Roman god of the sea.
   - ○ C
   - □ I
5. This planet travels the fastest through space.
   - ○ D
   - □ B
6. This planet has winters 21 years long.
   - ○ H
   - □ D
7. This planet is the smallest in the solar system.
   - ○ E
   - □ J
8. This planet has the largest moon.
   - ○ F
   - □ D
9. The surface of this planet is largely water.
   - ○ I
   - □ D
10. Seventeen moons orbit this planet.
   - ○ G
   - □ C

On Your Own

Keep your eye on the news. What new facts have astronomers discovered about our solar system? Keep a scrapbook of the discoveries you read about in newspapers and magazines.

The solar system has stored up these "out-of-the-world" facts.

- Mars has a salmon-pink daytime sky and a crystal-clear night sky.
- The closer a planet is to the Sun the faster it moves. Mercury speeds around the Sun at an amazing 127,000 miles per hour.
- Ganymede, one of Jupiter's sixteen moons, is the largest in our solar system. It is also larger than either of the planets Pluto or Mercury.
- The winters on Uranus are 21 years long. Temperatures get as low as -362 degrees F.
- Except for a 20-year period every 248 years, Pluto is the most distant planet from the sun.
- Believed to be a ball of frozen gas, Pluto is the smallest of all the planets and is even smaller than many moons.
- Oceans, ice caps, glaciers, lakes, rivers, and streams—over 70% of the Earth's surface is water.
- The Sun is the only star in our solar system. A huge ball of glowing gases, it is the only body in our solar system that generates its own light.
- The mysterious planet of Neptune with its two moons was named after the Roman god of the sea.
- Saturn, the gold-colored planet, has 17 moons and many known rings. It is one of the largest planets.

A. The Sun
B. Mercury
C. Venus
D. Earth
E. Mars

F. Jupiter
G. Saturn
H. Uranus
I. Neptune
J. Pluto

Answers

Moon Mistakes

Don't let these phony photos from a Moon journey fool you. Can you find the errors?

Our Moon is truly another world. It is different from Earth in many ways. The astronauts who have explored the Moon experienced some of its many differences. For example, because there is no air on the Moon to carry sound, the astronauts used radios to communicate with each other. And, because there is almost no gravity on the Moon, astronauts wore leaded boots. These prevented the astronauts from floating off the surface of the Moon.

To the right are scenes from an imaginary voyage to the Moon. Each scene contains one or more mistakes. The numbered sentences below each scene describe separate parts of that scene. Read each sentence and decide whether that part of the scene:

○ Actually happens on the Moon

☐ Does not happen on the Moon— a Moon mistake!

1. The stars twinkled in the black sky.   2. The astronaut could see Earth looking like a thin crescent.   3. She heard a loud crashing sound as her partner hammered a rock.   4. Looking at the lunar horizon, the astronaut realized that it was not as flat as Earth's horizon.

5. The astronauts noticed that a slight breeze caused their flag to wave.   6. They tested the lunar vehicle, which had an engine like a car.   7. They used a compass to navigate.

8. Both astronauts weighed less on the Moon.   9. They were able to jump higher than on Earth.   10. When the astronauts completed their research, they prepared for their seven-hour journey home.

What an exciting trip to the Moon! Remember looking beyond the curved horizon of the Moon to the Earth? We were surprised to see the crescent-shaped Earth just floating in the darkness!

Yes, it was a different view of the Earth. We were eager to step onto the moon after the long three-day journey. How light we felt—only one-sixth of our weight on Earth! You started hopping around like a kangaroo!

That was fun! It was strange to see you hammering on a rock without making any noise. With no air on the Moon, no sound can travel. With no breeze, the flag had to be stretched out with a special rod.

Then we went for a trip in our lunar vehicle. What a ride! Unlike an engine on Earth, our engine was designed to work without oxygen. Our computerized instruments helped guide us. Because there is no magnetic field on the Moon, a compass is useless.

Wouldn't it be great to make a return trip? I remember that magnificent view of the stars from the lunar rover. With no atmosphere on the Moon there was no twinkling at all.

That was a memorable trip! I do hope we can go back soon to learn more about Earth's closest neighbor.

On Your Own

Many Moon words and phrases are based on Moon fact and fiction. Tell whether these are based on fact or fantasy: "once in a blue moon," "the moon is made of green cheese," "make a wish on a new moon," "lunatic," "moon-struck," and "werewolves."

Answers

Sun Power

Picture this beach picnic without the Sun. Would it still be possible?

The Sun is the source of almost all the light, heat, and energy on Earth. All life—human, animal, and plant—depends on it. The Sun looks small to us because it is about 93 million miles away. (It would take 193 years to drive there at 55 m.p.h.) Even from that distance, the Sun can burn people! Have you ever had a sunburn?

The Earth receives only a tiny portion of the huge amount of light and heat generated by the hot gases on the Sun's surface. But this energy is still enough to produce most of our resources and material goods.

Look at the beach scene on the right. Decide whether or not each of the numbered things in the scene is available to us because of the Sun's energy. Decide if each object is:

○ Available because of the Sun's energy

□ Available even <u>without</u> the Sun's energy

Sometimes we think of our Sun as a light that shuts off at night. But if the Sun was really shut off, life as we know it would disappear in a short time.

We would run out of food quickly because plants need the Sun's heat and light to grow. Without plants there would be no trees for fruit, and no grains for bread or for cattle to eat. The cattle, in turn, would not be able to provide milk or meat.

We would also have no plants to provide pulp for paper or cotton for cloth.

Without the Sun, oil would not have developed. That's because oil is made from the remains of once-living plants. Millions of years ago, these plants used the Sun to make their food. After the plants died, they decomposed and compressed into layers of plants and soil. Slowly, these plant layers changed into the substance we call petroleum. Many plastic products, such as plastic toys, are made from petroleum.

Without the Sun there would be no wind or waves. The Sun heats the air and causes it to move. This wind causes waves to form on the ocean surface.

The Sun also causes water from the ocean to evaporate and gather into clouds of water vapor. Eventually rain and snow fall from the clouds. As the water runs downhill, it slowly breaks up rock, forming smaller rocks and sand. It forms rivers that provide fresh drinking water.

If there was no Sun, we would have almost none of the things we're used to. In fact, we wouldn't even be here!

On Your Own

There are places on Earth where there is very little sunlight for months at a time. Write a story about how your life would be different if you lived in such a sunless place.

Answers

Destination: Moon

Follow the steps of the first Moon travelers!

n July 16, 1969 Astronauts Neil Armstrong, Buzz Aldrin, and Michael Collins climbed into the Apollo 11 Command Module at the tip of the huge Saturn V Rocket. They were getting ready to go a long distance—to the Moon and back!

The pictures on the right show ten events of the Apollo 11 flight to the Moon. Read the captions under the pictures. In what order did the events take place? Put the pictures in order from one (first) to ten (last). Choose the letter that shows the correct order of each picture.

1. First
   - ○ E   ☐ D
2. Second
   - ○ F   ☐ C
3. Third
   - ○ H   ☐ D
4. Fourth
   - ○ A   ☐ E
5. Fifth
   - ○ F   ☐ J
6. Sixth
   - ○ B   ☐ H
7. Seventh
   - ○ G   ☐ C
8. Eighth
   - ○ J   ☐ G
9. Ninth
   - ○ J   ☐ I
10. Tenth
   - ○ I   ☐ B

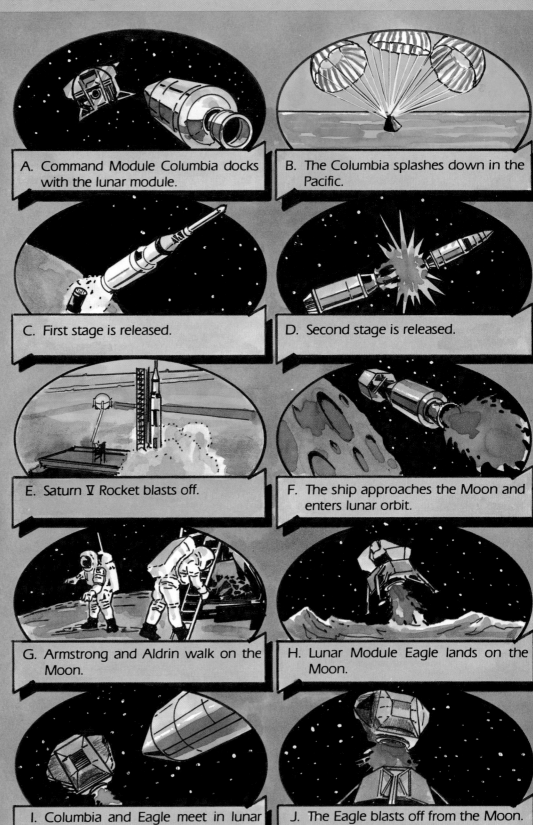

A. Command Module Columbia docks with the lunar module.

B. The Columbia splashes down in the Pacific.

C. First stage is released.

D. Second stage is released.

E. Saturn V Rocket blasts off.

F. The ship approaches the Moon and enters lunar orbit.

G. Armstrong and Aldrin walk on the Moon.

H. Lunar Module Eagle lands on the Moon.

I. Columbia and Eagle meet in lunar orbit.

J. The Eagle blasts off from the Moon.

Sun-Times
JULY 16 1969

Rocket Blasts Off For Moon

Kennedy Space Center, Florida—An excited crowd watched as the gigantic Saturn Rocket lifted off here at 9:32 a.m. Apollo 11 Astronauts Neil Armstrong, Edwin Aldrin, and Michael Collins hope to be the first humans to reach the Moon. Scientists cheered as the first two of the rocket's three stages fell away. The rocket went into Earth orbit and then headed out towards the Moon. Pilot Collins skillfully docked the command module with the lunar module, which had been inside the Saturn's third stage. The rest of the third stage was released. The crew members are now on their way.

Sun-Times
JULY 20 1969

Eagle Lands On Moon

The Columbia Command Module is now orbiting the Moon. Earlier today, Astronauts Armstrong and Aldrin put on pressure suits, left the Columbia, and floated into the lunar module, Eagle. The Eagle separated from the Columbia, unfolded its landing gear, and landed on the Moon. Pilot Collins remained in the Columbia, orbiting the Moon.

Inside the Eagle, Armstrong and Aldrin put on backpacks containing portable life-support systems. Television viewers around the world watched eagerly as Armstrong climbed down a ladder onto the Moon's surface. "That's one small step for man, one giant leap for mankind," he said as he stepped onto the Moon's surface.

Sun-Times
JULY 21 1969

Astronauts Head Home

The Eagle Lunar Module blasted off from the Moon yesterday and brought the two moonwalking astronauts back to the ship Columbia. The Eagle was left in Moon orbit, and the command module is now headed back to Earth, where a parade and a warm welcome await its three crew members.

Sun-Times
JULY 24 1969

Astronauts Arrive Home After Historic Moon Landing

The Columbia re-entered Earth's atmosphere today after its eight days in space. Small parachutes slowed the capsule's fall before it dropped safely into the Pacific Ocean. A U.S. Navy frogman from the aircraft carrier Hornet met Armstrong, Aldrin, and Collins in the first of many welcomes planned for the Apollo 11 crew.

Spacewalker Connections

Can you untangle these astronauts' cords before time runs out?

ince 1965 astronauts have been "walking" in space. Today's skywalkers can move freely outside their ships without any cords. Special jet packs, called MMU's, contain everything astronauts need to survive and maneuver in space.

Earlier astronauts, however, were connected to their spaceships by special cords. These cords not only saved the astronauts from flying helplessly into space, they contained vital communication lines, oxygen tubes and cooling systems.

In the imaginary picture to the right, you can see 10 astronauts—both with and without cords. With so much space traffic, some of them have gotten their cords tangled. Can you figure out their original connections?

For each numbered astronaut, follow the cord and decide if it is:

○ Connected to Spaceship A
△ Connected to Spaceship B
□ Not connected at all

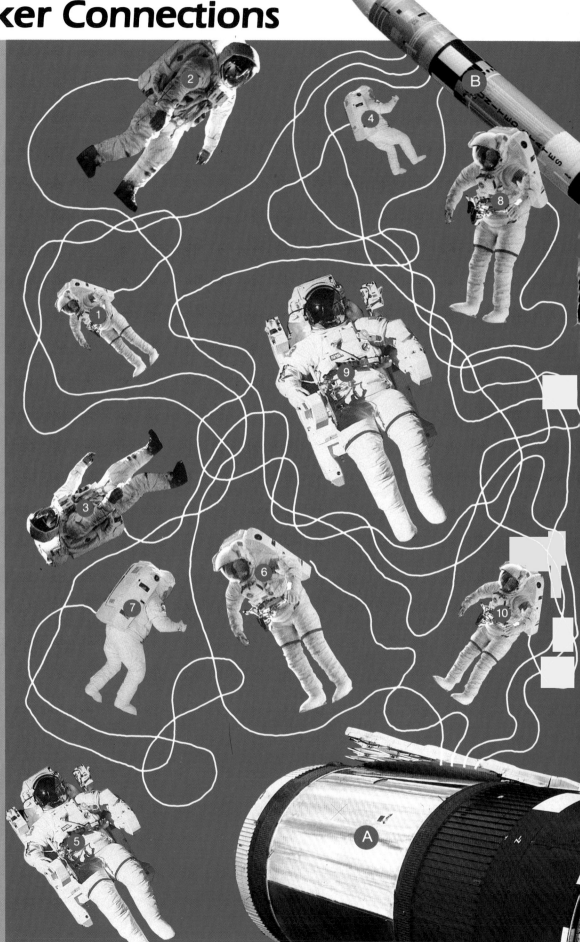

24

Free-Flying Spacewalk

The MANNED MANEUVERING UNIT (MMU) allows an astronaut, for the first time, to "walk" free in space. Imagine flying up to 45 m.p.h. with your own jet pack! You would be powered by 24 gas jets—almost like a mini-spaceship. The controls for the jet pack are in the armrest and can move you in any direction. Without a cord, you could zoom far out in space, filming the sights with the camera mounted on your space-age helmet. In the future, you could travel to repair a crippled satellite or to build an orbiting space station.

On Your Own

Write down six ways you might find an MMU useful in your life at school, at home, or on vacation. Draw a picture of your ideas and write a caption for each.

Invent a game you and your friends could play if you each had a MMU that worked on Earth.

Answers

Quest for Flight

Chart the course of flight—from shaky beginnings to soaring space achievements.

rom earliest times, people have dreamed of flying like the birds. They had no wings, but they had imaginations! In time they created machines that could lift off the ground and into the air. Did these early aviators guess that one day people would even fly in outer space?

On this page are lettered pictures of ten important flight inventions. Put them in order of their development, beginning with the earliest idea and ending with the most modern invention.

1. First
○ I   △ D   □ E
2. Second
○ I   △ J   □ E
3. Third
○ F   △ J   □ D
4. Fourth
○ G   △ H   □ J
5. Fifth
○ J   △ H   □ E
6. Sixth
○ H   △ F   □ G
7. Seventh
○ G   △ A   □ B
8. Eighth
○ H   △ C   □ G
9. Ninth
○ A   △ G   □ B
10. Tenth
○ B   △ E   □ C

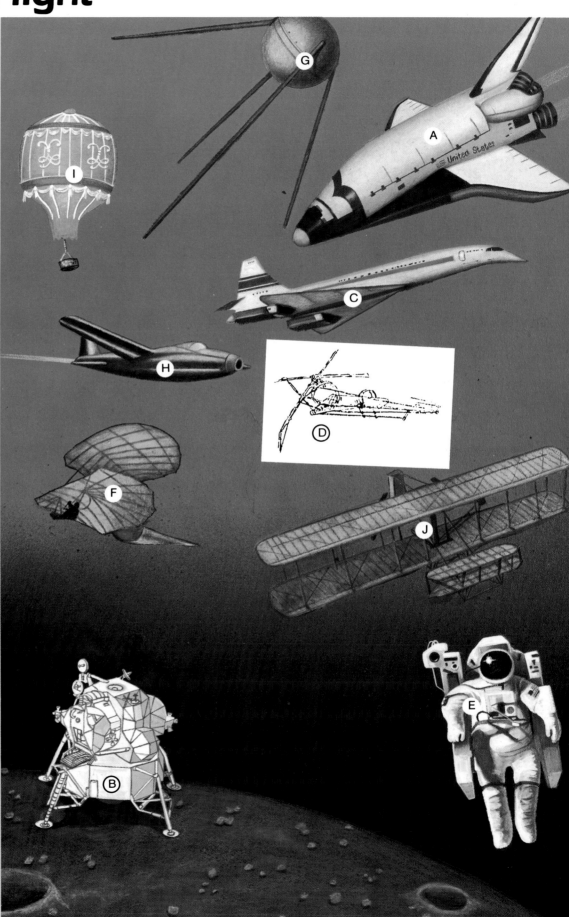

1500's—Leonardo da Vinci, Italian artist and inventor, made drawings of flying machines. He imagined a machine with flapping wings.

1783—A hot-air balloon, made by the Montgolfier brothers, carried the first humans into the air over Paris, France.

1890's—The first person to pilot a glider successfully in the air was Otto Lilienthal of Germany.

1903—The first engine-driven airplane, built by Wilbur and Orville Wright, flew for 12 seconds. It flew 120 feet at 30 m.p.h.

1939—The first successful flight of a jet airplane took place in Germany. It could fly as fast as 550 m.p.h., but could only carry enough fuel for a 10-minute flight.

1957—Sputnik launched the Space Age! Russia developed this first artificial satellite to orbit the Earth.

1969—The Apollo 11 spaceship was the first manned mission to land on the Moon. During their stay, American astronauts made an historic Moonwalk.

1976—The Concorde, built by France and Britain, was the first commercial supersonic transport plane. It flies at speeds greater than 660 m.p.h.—faster than the speed of sound!

1981—The Space Shuttle "Columbia" was the first reusable spacecraft. After its mission, it flew back to Earth and landed on a runway like a glider.

1984—The MMU, Manned Maneuvering Unit, allows an astronaut to fly freely in space for the first time. It is a jet backpack that can go up to 45 m.p.h.

On Your Own

Design a variety of airplanes out of paper. Which of your designs flies farthest, fastest, or highest? Why? Look for books in the library on paper airplanes that will help you apply the principles of aerodynamics to improve your designs.

Answers

Constellation Match-up

Find the starring characters in these sky stories!

eople from earliest times saw animals and people in patterns made by stars of the night sky. They made up stories to explain how these creatures got there.

Below is a list of names of ten constellations. In the boxes at the bottom of the page, each of the ten constellations is drawn with connecting lines. On the top of the page, the same constellations are shown as they would appear in the sky. Can you tell which constellation is which? Choose the correct letter.

1. Leo, the Lion
   ○ J   ☐ C
2. Little Bear
   ○ F   ☐ A
3. Gemini, the Twins
   ○ H   ☐ D
4. Orion, the Great Hunter
   ○ C   ☐ J
5. Cassiopeia, the Lady in Her Chair
   ○ G   ☐ A
6. Hercules, the Hero
   ○ I   ☐ E
7. Pegasus, the Winged Horse
   ○ I   ☐ G
8. Pleiades, the Seven Sisters
   ○ B   ☐ A
9. Great Bear
   ○ J   ☐ E
10. Cancer, the Crab
    ○ D   ☐ C

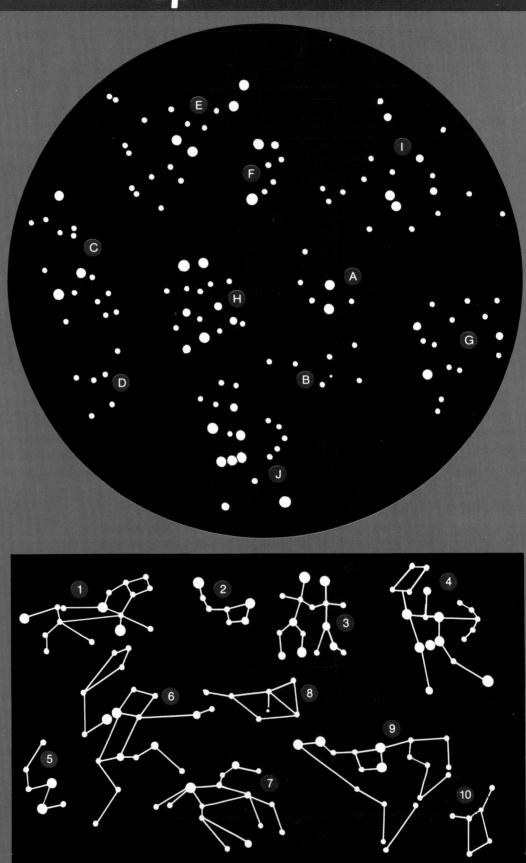

Thousands of years ago the Greeks saw the same constellations we do. Here is a sample of some of the legends they told about them.

Cassiopeia, the Lady in Her Chair

Cassiopeia had an honored place in the sky, but the Sea Nymphs complained to Poseidon that she was vain and didn't deserve it. So Poseidon had her sit on her throne for half the night, but hang upside down for the other half.

On Your Own

Use a star chart from your library to help you locate some of the constellations shown on this page. Easy ones to spot all year around are the Great and Little Bears and Cassiopeia.

Leo, the Lion

Leo was King of Beasts because no arrow could pierce his tough hide. But Hercules crushed Leo to death and used his skin for a suit of armor. The gods took pity on Leo and gave him a place in the stars.

Hercules, the Hero

Hercules was known for his great strength. He was made a god and was placed in the sky after he had performed twelve labors.

Great Bear and Little Bear

Hera, the wife of Zeus, was jealous of the beautiful Callisto. To protect Callisto, Zeus changed her into a big bear. He changed her son, Arcas, into a bear, too, and threw them both into the sky. The Big and Little Dippers are part of the Great Bear and Little Bear constellations.

Pegasus, the Winged Horse

The hero Bellerophon tamed Pegasus with a golden bridle. But when Bellerophon became proud, Zeus told Pegasus to throw him off. Then Zeus turned Pegasus into a constellation.

Answers

Gemini, the Twins

Castor and Pollux, twin sons of Zeus, were always together. When Castor was killed, Pollux asked Zeus to let him stay with his brother. Zeus placed the twins in the sky.

Pleiades, the Seven Sisters

Zeus placed the seven daughters of Atlas in the heavens to keep them safe from Orion, who had pursued them for seven years.

Orion, the Great Hunter

Apollo was angry with his sister Artemis and tricked her into killing the hunter Orion, whom she loved. When she saw what she had done, she carried Orion's body into the sky in her chariot.

Cancer, the Crab

The goddess Hera was jealous of Hercules and sent Cancer the Crab to nip him. When Hercules killed the crab, Hera felt sorry for it and placed it in the sky.

Home Away From Home

Imagine living and working in outer space!

Today scientists are working to develop a space station where crew members will live and work for months at a time. The crew members will use jet packs to travel to separate orbiting platforms for special research. They will work on products that are hard or impossible to make on Earth, such as some kinds of medicines.

As they go about their work and recreation, the crew members will get used to the lack of gravity.

To the right are scenes from ten compartments aboard a space station. Some show things that could happen in space. Others show things that could not happen. Can you tell which of the ten scenes are possible and which are impossible? Watch out! The numbers on the scenes are mixed-up.

For each numbered scene, decide if it:
- ○ Could happen in space
- ☐ Could not happen in space

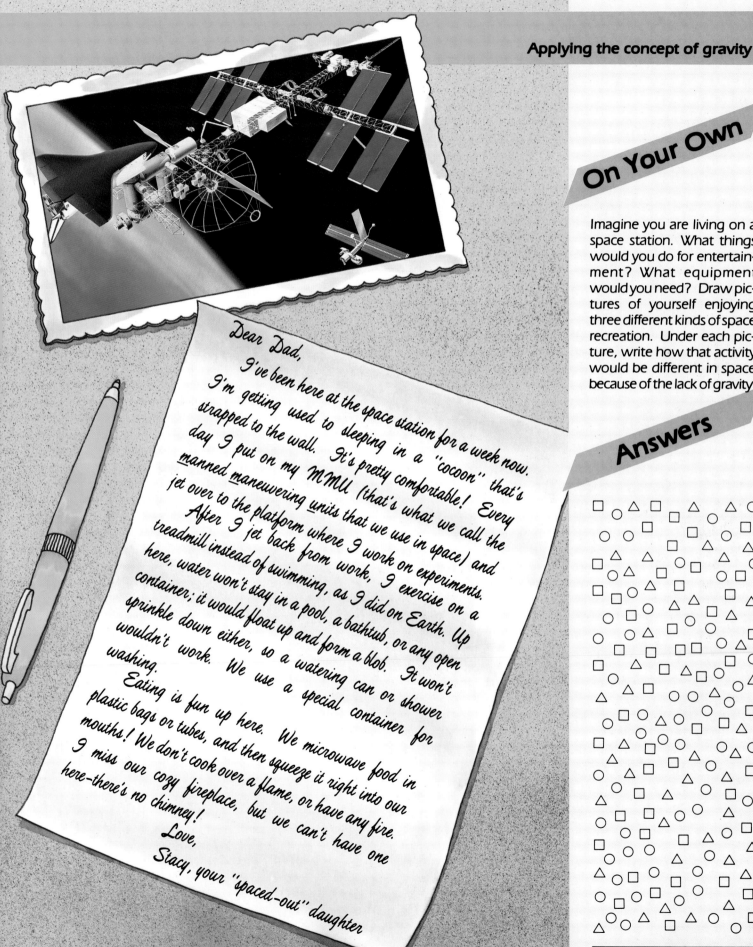

On Your Own

Imagine you are living on a space station. What things would you do for entertainment? What equipment would you need? Draw pictures of yourself enjoying three different kinds of space recreation. Under each picture, write how that activity would be different in space because of the lack of gravity.

Answers

Dear Dad,
I've been here at the space station for a week now. I'm getting used to sleeping in a "cocoon" that's strapped to the wall. It's pretty comfortable! Every day I put on my MMU (that's what we call the manned maneuvering units that we use in space) and jet over to the platform where I work on experiments.
After I jet back from work, I exercise on a treadmill instead of swimming, as I did on Earth. Up here, water won't stay in a pool, a bathtub, or any open container; it would float up and form a blob. It won't sprinkle down either, so a watering can or shower wouldn't work. We use a special container for washing.
Eating is fun up here. We microwave food in plastic bags or tubes, and then squeeze it right into our mouths! We don't cook over a flame, or have any fire. I miss our cozy fireplace, but we can't have one here—there's no chimney!
Love,
Stacy, your "spaced-out" daughter